This Book Belongs To:

_____

A Hawai'i Japanese New Year with Yuki-chan

A Hawai'i
Japanese New Year
with Yuki-chan

written by Tokie Ching

illustrated by Kerina Salazar

Mutual Publishing

All rights reserved.
ISBN-10: 1-56647-641-0
ISBN-13: 978-1-56647-641-6

Library of Congress Catalog Card
Number: 2003109948

First Printing, November 2003
Second Printing, October 2004
Third Printing, October 2005
Fourth Printing, September 2009

Mutual Publishing, LLC
1215 Center Street, Suite 210
Honolulu, Hawaii 96816
Ph: (808) 732-1709
Fax: (808) 734-4094
email: info@mutualpublishing.com
www.mutualpublishing.com

Printed in Taiwan

Acknowledgments

This book is lovingly dedicated to my daughter, Shan Yukie Matsumoto, for the endless joy and happiness she brings into our family. When she first arrived from Japan as a little girl, she gave me a deeper appreciation of the Japanese New Year's traditions and inspired me to write about them.

Special thanks go to my son, Grant Wilfred Ching, for all the encouragement, support, positive guidance, and technical assistance he provided me in seeing this book to completion. He was always there to offer me his expertise when I needed his advice.

Many thanks and gratitude to my husband, Wilfred Woody Ching, who patiently put up with the long nights that I spent writing and revising my story on the computer.

To my mom and dad, Kimie and Kazuto Ikeda, who taught me the value of courage, hard work, and determination in attaining my goals. They instilled in me the importance of the traditions of the Japanese New Year.

To my teammate, Charlene Ishimoto, who encouraged me to write about the Japanese New Year.

A great big mahalo to my illustrator, Kerina Salazar, for her eternal enthusiasm and effort in illustrating the book.

Special thanks to Sets Arai, who graciously shared her time to give us pertinent advice for the authenticity of the illustrations.

Much appreciation and deep gratitude to Jane Hopkins, Production Director, for patiently shepherding me through the publication process.

A big mahalo to the many people who assisted me to locate resource material and checked the story for accuracy.

I offer a challenge to the children who read this book to enjoy and continue the Japanese traditions so that they, too, can have the happiest New Year ever!

"Look at my white hands, Mom!" Yuki was drawing swirly lines through the powdery, white potato starch on Auntie Aileen's kitchen table. "This is how I came on the airplane from Japan to Hawai'i. I was really scared, but also excited to come live with my new family."

Mom made a big dot in the potato starch with her finger. "We were waiting for you right here at the airport. We were so excited to see you, too! When the gate opened, we saw a cute, little girl in a pretty, red dress with nine white buttons down the front. You wore matching red socks and white T-strapped sandals. Your cheeks were rosy pink and your short hair was jet-black. Oh, and when you smiled, your entire face lit up."

Yuki looked down at the picture her mom drew in the starch, and hugged herself.

"Tears rolled down my cheeks when you ran to me, gave me a big hug, and called me Mommy!" said Mom.

Yuki stretched her arms open wide and gave her mom the biggest hug ever.

It was a week before New Year's Day, and here she stood with her new mom in Auntie Aileen's house getting ready for the celebration.

"Now, let's get started. Making *mochi* is the first thing we do to get ready for the New Year," said Mom.

Yuki was excited. She had never celebrated New Year's with a family before and looked forward to the tasty Japanese food they would prepare.

Gatan, gatan, gatan, pounded the *mochi*-maker. "Watch out, the *mochi* is very hot," said cousin Laura, as she carefully poured the hot, steamy, sticky *mochi* on top of the potato starch covering the huge cutting board.

Auntie Aileen molded one great, big, round *mochi* and then a smaller one to make a set of *kagami mochi.* She carefully placed the smaller one on top of the big one.

"What's that for?" asked Yuki.

"The mochi symbolizes longevity," Auntie Aileen said. "We hope that we will have another happy, healthy and safe year. Okay, Yuki, now it's your turn to mold the smaller *mochi.* Remember, if you make it round and smooth, you will have a trouble-free new year."

Yuki tried to make it round, but the *mochi* was sticking to her palms.

"Pat some more potato starch on your hands," suggested cousin Laura.

Yuki rolled and rolled the dough in her hands. In a few moments, she made a perfect, little round ball and flattened it. "Hooray!" Yuki shouted. "I did it!"

"Good job," said Auntie Tomi, "but look in the mirror." Yuki turned to see herself covered with white potato starch from head to toe. She looked like a ghost! Everyone laughed.

Several days before the year end, Yuki asked Mom, "What else can we do to get ready for the New Year?"

"Today," Mom said, "we must clean our home until it is spotless. *Osoji* is just like spring-cleaning. We wipe away any trace of bad luck left in the house."

Yuki and Mom cleaned the kitchen and Buddha's altar. Yuki polished the candlesticks until they were so shiny she could see her face in them. Dad polished the windows and cleaned the screens. Yuki's brother, Grant, vacuumed the entire house. When they were done, their home looked and smelled fresh and clean. They were ready for the New Year.

Mom carefully placed the *kagami mochi* on a special paper called *saiwaigami*. Pictures of Mt. Fuji, a hawk, and an eggplant were on it to bring strength and long life to their family. Mom let Yuki put the roundest and most brightly colored tangerine with three leaves on the very top of the *kagami mochi*.

"We want our family," Mom said, "to have good wishes for a wonderful life in the New Year."

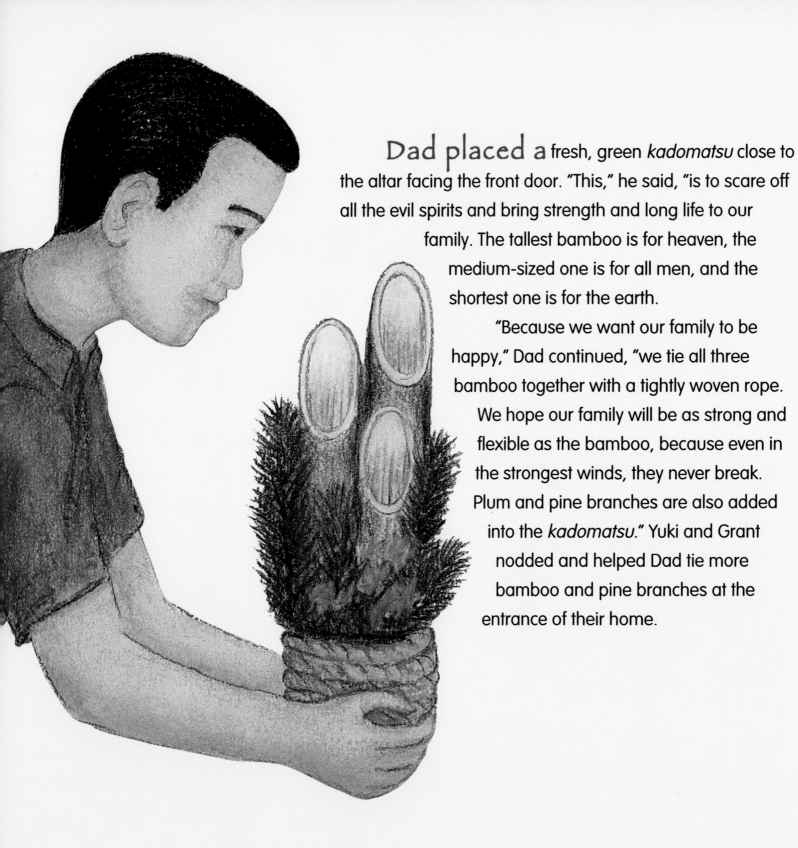

Dad placed a fresh, green *kadomatsu* close to the altar facing the front door. "This," he said, "is to scare off all the evil spirits and bring strength and long life to our family. The tallest bamboo is for heaven, the medium-sized one is for all men, and the shortest one is for the earth.

"Because we want our family to be happy," Dad continued, "we tie all three bamboo together with a tightly woven rope. We hope our family will be as strong and flexible as the bamboo, because even in the strongest winds, they never break. Plum and pine branches are also added into the *kadomatsu*." Yuki and Grant nodded and helped Dad tie more bamboo and pine branches at the entrance of their home.

Next, Dad pulled out a long rope with white paper lightning bolts hanging from it.

"Why are you putting those zigzag papers above the door?" Grant asked. "Will they keep the evil spirits away, too?"

"They sure will," said Dad. "We hang these strips of paper on this *shimenawa* to stop the bad spirits from entering our home. The *shimenawa* is a very special piece of rope made from straw."

When they finished, they stood and admired their work. All the special decorations inside their home made them feel very safe.

The New Year was a few hours away. That evening, Yuki tried to stay awake. There was no way she was going to miss the evening's celebrations. Finally, Mom made the announcement.

"It's one hour before midnight," Mom said. "Time to go to the temple and hear the midnight tolling of the bells."

"I remember hearing *joya no kane* in Japan. It is really fun!" said Yuki as she rushed to get ready.

Many of their friends were already at the church when they arrived.

First, they bowed to the Buddha. Then Dad lifted Yuki up so she could reach the large, heavy, wooden hammer hanging next to the bell. She swung with all her might, and as the hammer hit the side, the *tsurugane* made a loud bonnnnnnng! Yuki covered her ears and smiled.

Mom called Yuki and Grant to her. "Buddhist people believe that the year should start with a pure heart. The ringing of the bell signifies that purity. At midnight, the bell will ring one hundred times."

Yuki couldn't believe it. One hundred seemed like a lot.

The bell rang eight times before midnight. Yuki looked at her watch. At the stroke of twelve, the bell began to ring. Yuki and Grant covered their ears and patiently waited and counted... ...97, 98, 99, and finally 100! "*Hyaku*!" Yuki shouted.

Everyone exchanged greetings. "Happy New Year! S*hinnen omedeto gozaimasu*!"

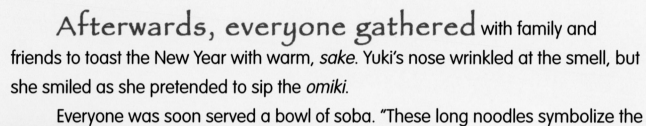

Afterwards, everyone gathered with family and
friends to toast the New Year with warm, *sake*. Yuki's nose wrinkled at the smell, but
she smiled as she pretended to sip the *omiki*.

Everyone was soon served a bowl of soba. "These long noodles symbolize the
long life we hope to have," explained Mom.

"They're delicious!" Grant exclaimed.

"Mmm, *oishii!*" Yuki exclaimed.

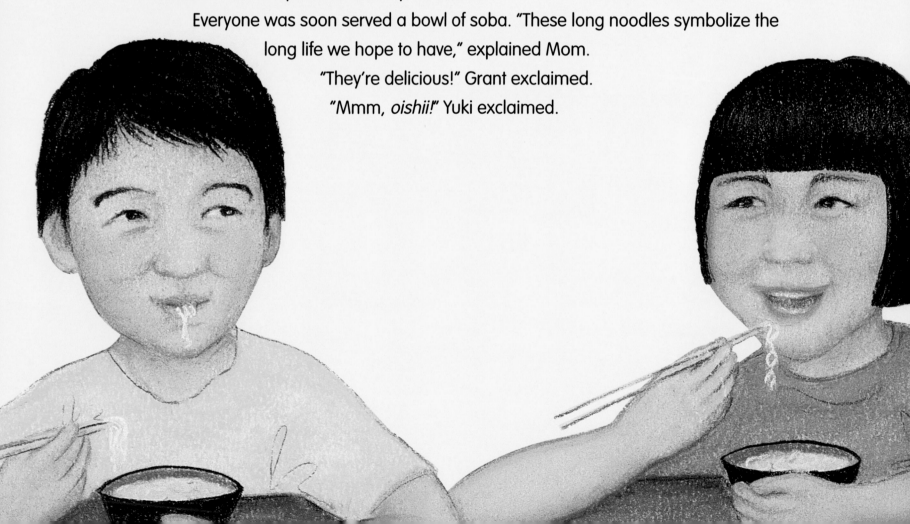

On the way home, Yuki sang a special New Year song she had learned in Japan.

"What do the words mean?" Grant asked.

"New Year will be here when I sleep another night. We will fly our kites and spin our tops. Come quickly, New Year!" answered Yuki.

Yuki taught her new family the song. They had lots of fun singing all the way home.

17

When they got home, Mom said that it would be a good sign if they dreamed of a hawk, Mt. Fuji, or an eggplant. "Good night, everyone," Yuki said. "*Oyasumi nasai!*"

Everyone hoped that they would have good dreams as they went to sleep.

"*Ohayo gozaimasu*!" Mom said cheerfully later that morning. "Rise and shine!"

Yuki sat up and rubbed her eyes. It was still dark out. "It's not morning, yet," she said, confused.

"You must get up early to see the first sunrise of the year, " said Mom. We must be happy today because this is how you want to be for the rest of the year."

Yuki and Grant were very sleepy, but they slowly got out of bed and tried to put smiles on their faces.

Mom had the tub ready for *asa buro*. She explained that a morning bath is taken to wash away old traces of bad luck from the past year. "Remember to wash behind your ears and between your toes," she said.

After Yuki and Grant put on their new clothes, they felt more awake. They were ready to welcome in the New Year. Outside, in the cool air, they stood with their parents and saw the first sunrise of the year. It was beautiful.

19

"Your *ozoni* soup is ready," Mom said as they came in the house. She had gotten up very early to prepare this special, traditional New Year soup. It smelled delicious. "*Itadakimasu!*" Yuki exclaimed.

Yuki had fun pulling the sticky *mochi* in the *ozoni* soup between her teeth. "Mmm," she said, "I remember this taste. It's delicious."

Mom explained that the stickiness that holds the *mochi* together symbolized their hope that their family would be together for a long time.

While Yuki was enjoying the *mochi*, Grant was chomping on the colorful *kamaboko*. Dad told them that the red and white of the fishcake is a lucky color combination that will bring them happiness.

The four of them enjoyed the *ozoni* as their first meal of the year together.

Mom had worked very hard before New Year preparing the foods that would bring them good luck in the future. Because *osechi ryori* takes place before New Year's Day, all the cooking was already done and Mom could enjoy this special day, too.

Sushi was Yuki's favorite food of the New Year. She sat and watched Mom scoop vinegared rice onto strips of black seaweed called *nori.* Mom then twirled long strips of dried turnip called *kanpyo* around her fingers and on the cutting board, finely sliced red *kamaboko,* green watercress, and a thin, fried omelet to add to the *Kanpyo* and *unagi.* Yuki clapped her hands in excitement when her favorite was prepared—the *unagi*—canned eel.

Mom carefully placed all of the ingredients directly in the center of the rice and rolled the *sushi* with a bamboo mat. It was very colorful and looked like a jellyroll. Yuki couldn't wait to taste it.

"First, to be healthy the whole year," Mom said, "everyone must have a spoonful of *kuromame.* '*Kuro*' means black and '*mame de kurasu*' means living in good health." She had cooked the black beans in a sweet sauce for a long time. Grant made a face as Mom placed the pretty lacquered bowl of beans on the table. Beans were definitely not his favorite, but he held his breath and gobbled one down.

"Wow," he said, "I feel healthy already."

Everyone laughed.

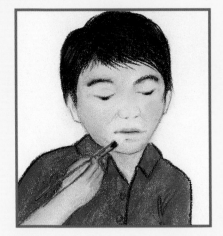

Dad's eyes got big when Mom started to serve his favorite *nishime*. "This vegetable dish," Mom said, "has many interesting ingredients." She scooped out a lotus root that had many holes in it. "In Japan," she explained, "this is called *hasu*. It looks like the wheel of life which is very special in the Buddhist religion."

Next she scooped a piece of round potato out of the *nishime*. It rolled around in the spoon. "*Imo*," she said, "is eaten to drive away all the evil spirits and bring good fortune to us."

"I need one of those," said Grant. Mom put the potato on his plate and he eagerly ate it. "Mmmm," he said, "it's so soft and yummy."

"These," Mom said as she picked two more ingredients out of the *nishime*, "are turnip and burdock."

"What are they for?" Yuki asked.

"*Daikon* and *gobo*," Mom answered, "grow with their roots deep in the ground. When we eat them, we hope our family will deeply love and care for one another."

Everyone, especially Dad, enjoyed the *nishime*. But Grant's favorite wasn't the *nishime* — it was *sashimi*. Mom served him a heaping portion of the raw fish and told them that it would bring lots of good luck.

"I think I have sand in my mouth," Yuki said as she ate some of the *sashimi.* Mom laughed and said, "Those are the eggs of the fish. *Kazunoko* are very special because they mean that our family will be blessed with many children, and that our grandchildren will enjoy long and prosperous lives."

"That looks like a Japanese hot dog," Yuki said as Mom put a sausage-shaped dish on her plate. Mom laughed and said, "It's not a hot dog. *Konbumaki* is seaweed wrapped around fish. In Japanese, *kobu* means happiness and *maki* means to wrap around."

"*Oishii*," said Yuki as she ate it. It tasted so good.

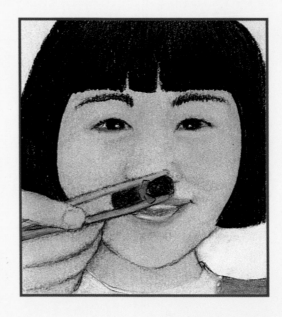

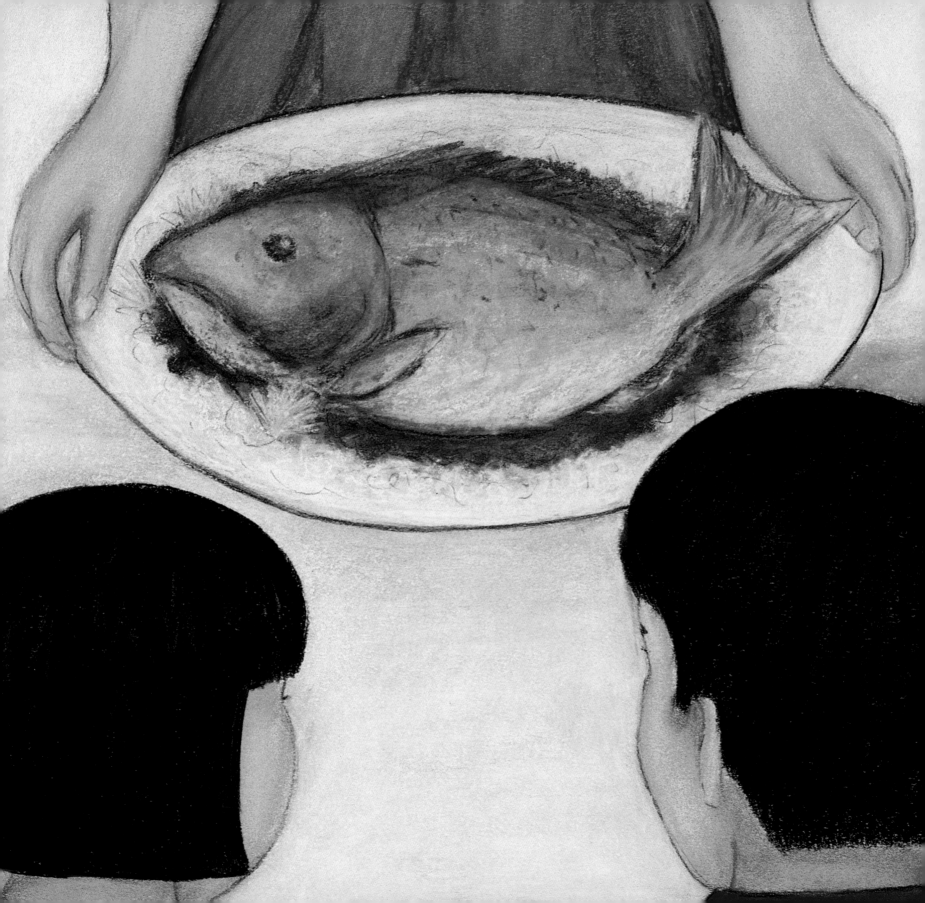

On another large platter, in the middle of the table, was a beautiful red kingfish called *tai*. It lay on a net made of turnip. While Mom served it, she said, "When this is served together with all the other food during New Year, it shows that everyone will be able to work and live peacefully together."

When the *tai* was almost gone, everyone sat back in their chairs and sighed. They were so full from eating all the delicious dishes. But, there was still one more left. It was Mom's favorite — *hoshi gaki*. "I've waited a whole year to eat this," she said.

"What is it?" Yuki asked. She had never seen *hoshi gaki* before. "This," Mom said as she gave Yuki some, "is dried persimmon. Persimmon is a fruit that comes from Japan only during the New Year. It is sweet, soft, and very delicious." Yuki took a bite and exclaimed, "*Oishii!*"

"But," Mom said, "the persimmon doesn't start out that way. When it's young and green, it tastes very bitter. It only becomes very sweet and delicious when it ripens. You see, Yuki, when you are young, you have lots to learn. And if you continue to study, as you get older, you will become a wiser, smarter, and better person."

Yuki nodded her head. Then she said, "*Gochiso sama deshita,* Mom. Thank you for all the delicious food!"

All day long, friends, neighbors, and relatives came over to exchange New Year greetings. Mom and Dad welcomed them in to have a bite to eat.

When Uncle Hiroshi, Uncle Hisashi, Uncle Mits, and Uncle Sus came over, they gave Yuki and Grant money in specially decorated New Year envelopes called *otoshidama.* "*Arigato gozaimasu,*" said Yuki to her uncles. "Thank you very much," said Grant.

At the end of the day, Yuki was very tired but also very happy. Even though she was now in Hawai'i and far from Japan, she was able to eat all of the Japanese foods she loved — and even some new ones like *hoshi gaki.* She also got to experience all of the traditions of Japanese New Year and learned many things about them that she didn't know before. She felt very lucky to be adopted into such a special family. She gave a big hug to Mom, Dad, and Grant and thanked them for such an exciting and fun New Year's Day, filled with both all of the things she loved about Japan and all of her new family. "*Arigato gozaimasu,*" she said and bowed.

"You can take Yuki out of Japan," Grant said, "but you can't take the love of Japan out of Yuki." Yuki smiled and said, "*Shinnen omedeto gozaimasu*! Happy New Year to all! This was my best New Year ever!"

Ozoni (New Year Soup)

Osumashi (Basic Clear Soup)
1 small can hokkigai, cut into 1/2-inch pieces
1/2 bunch Mizuna
8 to 10 pieces of mochi
18 thin slices of kamaboko

Make the osumashi (see recipe below). In another pot, boil 1/2 bunch of Mizuna in slightly salted water, drain and cut into 1-1/2 inch lengths. Place the mochi (softened in boiling water or broiled), a pinch of Mizuna, hokkigai, and 3 pieces of kamaboko into a lacquered soup bowl. Pour the boiling osumashi over all. Yield: 6 servings.

Osumashi (Basic Clear Soup)

5 cups water
1 pkg, Katsuo dashinomoto
1 Tablespoon shoyu
1 teaspoon salt

Add dashinomoto into a pot of boiling water. Add shoyu and salt and bring soup to a boil.

Konbu Maki

8 oz. Nishime konbu

1 pound pork, chicken or fish

Gobo, cut into 2-inch halves

1 package Kanpyo to tie (soften in water)

1/3 cup shoyu

1 teaspoon salt

3 Tablespoons sugar

2 Tablespoons mirin

Wash sand off konbu and cut into 5 to 6-inch lengths. Cut pork, chicken or fish into strips 1/2 x 1/2 x 2 1/2 inches. Place a piece of pork, chicken, or fish and gobo on one end of the konbu strip, roll and tie with Kanpyo (dried gourd). Put konbu maki in a sauce pan, add water to cover and cook until tender (about 3 hours). Add shoyu, salt, sugar, and mirin and cook for another 30 minutes.

Nishime

1 package nishime konbu (1 oz.)

1 medium burdock root (gobo)

1 teaspoon vinegar

1 cup water

10 araimo

1 can (6.5 oz.) bamboo shoots

1 small daikon

1 medium carrot

1/2 pound lotus root

1/4 cup iriko or 1 Tablespoon dashi base

3 pieces dried mushroom, soaked in 2 cups of water (save this mushroom water)

1 container konyaku (10 oz.), cut in 3/4 x 1 inch pieces

2 aburage, cut into 1-1/2 inch pieces

1/3 cup shoyu

2 teaspoons salt

2 Tablespoons sugar

Wash konbu and tie into knots at 2-inch intervals; cut between knots. Scrape gogo, cut diagonally in 1/4-inch slices. Add 1 teaspoon vinegar to 1 cup of water. Soak gobo in this solution for 10 minutes. Drain. Parboil araimo, unpeeled; drain. Remove skin and cut large ones in half. Cut bamboo shoots, daikon, and carrots into 1-inch pieces. Cut lotus root in to 1/4-inch slices.

Place iriko, or dashi base, at the bottom of a deep pot. Place mushrooms, konbu, and konyaku and add 2 cups of mushroom water. Cover and cook for 10 minutes.

Add carrots, turnips, gobo, bamboo shoots and aburage. Cover and cook for 15 minutes. Mix shoyu, salt and sugar together and pour over layers. Cover and bring to a boil. Lower to medium heat. Add araimo and lotus root. Cover and cook for 20 minutes or until all vegetables are cooked. Cool in pot. Mix gently and serve.

Glossary

Asa buro (ah-sah boo-roe): Morning bath.

Arigato gozaimasu (ah-ree-gah-TOE go-zie-mahss): "Thank you."

Daikon (dah-ee-koe-n): Turnip.

Gatan (gah-TAH-n): Sound of machine.

Gochiso sama (go-chee-SOE sah-mah): "Thank you for this delicious food."

Gobo (go-boe): Burdock.

Hasu (ha-sue): Lotus root.

Hoshi gaki (hoe-SHI ga-KEE): Dried persimmon.

Hyaku (he-ah-kue): One hundred.

Itadakimasu (ee-TAH-dah-kee-mahss): "I accept this food with gratefulness."

Joya no kane (ghee-yoe-yah no ka-ney): Tolling of the bells.

Kadomatsu (ka-doe-MAT-t'sue): Three bamboo tied together with pine and plum blossoms.

Kagami mochi (ka-gah-me moe-chee): Set of a large and small rice cake.

Kamaboko (ka-MA-boe-koe): Fish cake.

Kanpyo (KA-n-pee-yoe): Dried turnip.

Kazunoko (ka-ZOO-no-koe): Fish eggs.

Glossary

Konbumaki (koe-n-boo-mah-kee): Seaweed wrapped around fish.

Kuromame (kuu-ROE-mah-may): Black bean.

Mochi (moe-CHEE): Rice cake.

Nishime (nee-she-MAY): Cooked vegetable dish.

Ohayo gozaimasu (oh-hie-YOE go-zie-mahss): "Good morning."

Omiki (oh-me-kee): Warm rice wine.

Oishii (oh-ee-she): Delicious.

Osechi ryori (oh-say-chee ree-YO-ri): Preparation of New Year food.

Oshogatsu (oh-SHO-gah-t'sue): New Year.

Osoji (oh-so-jee): Housecleaning.

Otoshidama (oh-toe-she-dah-mah): Money in a New Year envelope.

Oyasumi nasai (oh-yah-sue-me nah-sie): "Good night."

Saiwaigami (sah-ee-wah-ee-gah-me): New Year paper on which the kazane mochi is placed.

Sashimi (sa-she-me): Sliced raw fish.

Shimenawa (she-may-nah-wah): Sacred circle-roped decorated with New Year ornaments.

Shinnen omedeto gozaimasu (SHIN-neyn oh-may-day-TOE go-zah-ee-mah-sue): "Happy New Year!"

Soba (SO-bah): Noodles.

Sushi (sue-she): Japanese vinegared rice.

Tai (tah-ee): Japanese kingfish.

Takenoko (tah-kay-no-koe): Bamboo shoot.

Tsurugane (t'sue-rue-gah-nay): Bell.

Unagi (uu-nah-ghee): Eel.

Note: The "R" sound in Japanese is close to the "L" sound in English.